CW01011665

www.booksbyboxer.com

Bee Three Publishing is an imprint of Books By Boxer
Published by
Books By Boxer, Leeds, LS13 4BS, UK
Books by Boxer (EU), Dublin, D02 P593, IRELAND
Boxer Gifts LLC, 955 Sawtooth Oak Cir, VA 22802, USA
© Books By Boxer 2024
All Rights Reserved
MADE IN CHINA
ISBN: 9781915410450

This book is produced from responsibly sourced paper to ensure forest management

ROAST CHICKEN

INGREDIENTS

- 1 WHOLE CHICKEN (MEDIUM SIZE)
- 1 TBSP. OLIVE OIL
- SALT AND PEPPER (TO TASTE)

METHOD

SERVES **6**

5 MINUTES PREP

50 MINUTES COOK

STEP 01 REMOVE THE BOTTOM SHELF AND GREASE THE BASE OF THE AIR FRYER DRAWER WITH OLIVE OIL.

STEP 02 PREHEAT THE AIR FRYER TO 180°C | 350°F.

STEP 03 RUB OLIVE OIL INTO THE TOP OF THE CHICKEN, AND SPRINKLE WITH YOUR DESIRED AMOUNT OF SALT AND PEPPER (YOU CAN ALSO ADD HERBS AND SPICES TO COMPLIMENT THE FLAVOR - WE SUGGEST ROSEMARY, GARLIC, AND LEMON!).

STEP 04 PLACE THE CHICKEN BREAST-SIDE DOWN INTO THE AIR FRYER AND COOK FOR 30 MINUTES.

STEP 05 TURN THE CHICKEN OVER AND COOK FOR ANOTHER 20-25 MINUTES (DEPENDING ON SIZE).

STEP 06 ALLOW THE CHICKEN TO REST FOR A FEW MINUTES BEFORE SERVING.

FRENCH TOAST

INGREDIENTS

> 4 SLICES WHITE BREAD
  (MEDIUM THICKNESS)
> 2 EGGS
> 80ML | 2 ¾ OZ MILK

METHOD

SERVES
4

10 MINUTES PREP

08 MINUTES COOK

STEP 01 CRACK THE EGGS INTO A BOWL, THEN ADD THE MILK AND WHISK UNTIL SMOOTH AND FROTHY (YOU COULD ALSO INTENSIFY THE FLAVOR WITH A DASH OF CINNAMON OR VANILLA EXTRACT).

STEP 02 PREHEAT THE AIR FRYER AT 180°C | 350°F.

STEP 03 SLICE THE BREAD IN HALF DIAGONALLY, THEN DIP ALL SLICES INTO THE MIXTURE UNTIL SOAKED.

STEP 04 ADD THE BREAD TO THE AIR FRYER DRAWER, WITH SPACE IN-BETWEEN EACH SLICE (BE CAREFUL NOT TO RIP THE BREAD).

STEP 05 COOK FOR 8 MINUTES, TURNING EACH SLICE OVER MIDWAY (YOU MIGHT NEED TO LEAVE THEM FOR ANOTHER MINUTE ON EACH SIDE IF NOT CRISP ENOUGH).

STEP 06 ENJOY YOUR FRENCH TOAST ON ITS OWN, OR ADD YOUR FAVORITE TOPPING!

TOP TIP WE LOVE POWDERED SUGAR AND STRAWBERRIES!

MEXICAN SHRIMP

INGREDIENTS

- 450G | 1 LB SHRIMP (READY TO COOK)
- 1 TBSP. OLIVE OIL
- 1 TSP. GROUND CUMIN
- 1 TSP. CHILI POWDER
- ½ TSP. PAPRIKA
- ½ TSP. GARLIC POWDER
- ½ TSP. DRIED OREGANO
- ½ TSP. SALT
- ¼ TSP. GROUND BLACK PEPPER

METHOD

SERVES 4 | 10 MINUTES PREP | 10 MINUTES COOK

STEP 01 IN A BOWL, ADD THE SHRIMP, OLIVE OIL, CUMIN, CHILI POWDER, PAPRIKA, OREGANO, GARLIC POWDER, SALT, AND PEPPER.

STEP 02 MOVE THE SHRIMP AROUND UNTIL COATED, AND ALLOW TO MARINATE FOR 10 MINUTES.

STEP 03 HEAT THE AIR FRYER AT 176°C | 350°F AND COOK THE SHRIMP FOR 8-10 MINUTES, SHAKING THE DRAWER HALFWAY THOUGH.

PORK CHOPS

INGREDIENTS

- 3 BONELESS PORK CHOPS
- 1 TBSP. OLIVE OIL
- 2 TSP. SEASONING (BASIL, OREGANO, ROSEMARY, AND THYME ARE GREAT CHOICES)
- 1 TSP. PAPRIKA
- SALT AND PEPPER (TO TASTE)

METHOD

STEP 01 PREHEAT THE AIR FRYER TO 190°C | 375°F, AND SPREAD A THIN LAYER OF OLIVE OIL IN THE DRAWER.

STEP 02 USING OLIVE OIL, BRUSH THE PORK CHOPS, THEN SPRINKLE EACH CHOP WITH PAPRIKA, SEASONING, AND SALT AND PEPPER.

STEP 03 PLACE THE CHOPS INTO THE AIR FRYER FOR 10-12 MINUTES, FLIPPING HALFWAY THROUGH.

TOP TIP WE SUGGEST SERVING WITH ROAST VEGETABLES AND SOME APPLE SAUCE TO REALLY ENHANCE THE FLAVOR!

FALAFEL SALAD

INGREDIENTS

- 2 CLOVES OF GARLIC
- 4 SPRING ONIONS (SCALLIONS)
- 780G | 6 ½ CUPS BABY KALE
- 2 CANS OF CHICKPEAS
- 1 TSP. GRATED LEMON ZEST
- 75G | ½ CUP CUCUMBER
- 2 TBSP. ALL-PURPOSE FLOUR
- 1 TSP. GROUND CUMIN
- 3 TBSP. OLIVE OIL
- 1 TSP. GROUND CORIANDER (CILANTRO)
- 127G | ¼ CUP FRESH MINT LEAVES
- KOSHER/ROCK SALT
- 2 TBSP. LEMON JUICE
- 125G | ½ CUP FRESH PARSLEY LEAVES

METHOD

SERVES 4 | 10 MINUTES PREP | 20 MINUTES COOK

STEP 01 BLEND TOGETHER SPRING ONION WHITES (KEEPING THE GREENS FOR LATER), GARLIC, AND ½ A CUP BABY KALE IN A FOOD PROCESSOR UNTIL CHOPPED FINELY.

STEP 02 ADD LEMON ZEST, FLOUR, CUMIN, CHICKPEAS, CORIANDER, AND ½ TSP. SALT TO THE MIXTURE AND BLEND AGAIN TO COMBINE.

STEP 03 ROLL THE MIXTURE INTO 24 BALLS (ABOUT 2 TBSP. OF MIXTURE FOR EACH BALL).

STEP 04 PREHEAT THE AIR FRYER TO 160°C | 325°F, AND EVENLY COAT THE DRAWER WITH OIL.

STEP 05 ADD THE FALAFEL BALLS AND AIR FRY FOR 15 MINUTES, THEN BRUSH THE BALLS WITH OIL.

STEP 06 INCREASE THE TEMPERATURE TO 200°C | 400°F, AND FRY FOR ANOTHER 5 MINUTES (OR UNTIL GOLDEN).

STEP 07 IN A BOWL, ADD 2 TBSP. OLIVE OIL AND LEMON JUICE AND MIX TOGETHER. ADD CUCUMBERS, BABY KALE, PARSLEY, GREENS FROM SPRING ONIONS, MINT AND ½ TSP. SALT.

STEP 08 TOSS THE SALAD WELL, AND ADD THE FALAFEL!

RIBEYE STEAK WITH GARLIC BUTTER

INGREDIENTS

> 2 RIBEYE STEAKS
> 2 TSP. SALT
> 1 TSP. GARLIC POWDER
> 1 ½ TSP. GROUND BLACK PEPPER
> 120G | ½ CUP BUTTER (SOFTENED)
> 1 GARLIC CLOVE CRUSHED
> 2 TSP. PARSLEY (FINELY CHOPPED)

METHOD

SERVES 2 | 10 MINUTES PREP | 8-12 MINUTES COOK

STEP 01 PREPARE THE GARLIC BUTTER BY MIXING THE BUTTER, CRUSHED GARLIC, AND PARSLEY TOGETHER. PREHEAT THE AIR FRYER TO 200°C | 400°F.

STEP 02 IN A SMALL BOWL, ADD SALT, GARLIC POWDER, AND PEPPER, THEN MIX.

STEP 03 COAT BOTH SIDES OF EACH STEAK WITH THE SEASONINGS, PRESSING THEM INTO THE STEAKS USING YOUR HAND.

STEP 04 PLACE STEAKS INTO THE AIR FRYER AND COOK FOR 7 MINUTES, FLIPPING HALFWAY.

STEP 05 WITHOUT OPENING THE AIR FRYER, TURN IT OFF AND WAIT:
- 1 MINUTES FOR RARE STEAK
- 3 MINUTES FOR MEDUIM STEAK
- 5 MINUTES FOR WELL DONE STEAK
(LEAVE IN AS LONG AS YOU PREFER)

STEP 06 TOP WITH GARLIC BUTTER AND SERVE!

CORNFLAKE CHICKEN NUGGETS

INGREDIENTS

- 230G | 8OZ BONELESS CHICKEN BREAST
- 30G | ¼ CUP CORNSTARCH
- ¼ TSP. PEPPER
- ¼ TSP. KOSHER/ROCK SALT
- ¼ TSP. GARLIC POWDER
- 60ML | ¼ CUP BUTTERMILK
- 60G | 2OZ FINELY CRUSHED CORNFLAKES

METHOD

SERVES 2 | **10 MINUTES PREP** | **10 MINUTES COOK**

STEP 01 DICE CHICKEN INTO 1 INCH (2.5CM) PIECES.

STEP 02 TAKE 3 BOWLS. ADD GARLIC POWDER, PEPPER, AND CORNSTARCH INTO THE 1ST BOWL.

STEP 03 ADD BUTTERMILK INTO THE 2ND BOWL, AND GROUND CORNFLAKES INTO THE 3RD BOWL.

STEP 04 SPRINKLE A LITTLE BIT OF SALT ONTO EACH CHICKEN PIECE, THEN ROLL THEM IN THE 1ST BOWL.

STEP 05 ADD THE CHICKEN TO THE 2ND BOWL, COVERING WELL AND ALLOWING THE EXCESS TO DRIP OFF.

STEP 06 ROLL THE CHICKEN THROUGH THE CORNFLAKES, COVERING WELL. SPRAY THE CHICKEN WITH COOKING OIL.

STEP 07 COOK THE CHICKEN AT 200°C | 400°F, TURNING THE PIECES HALFWAY THROUGH, FOR 8-10 MINUTES (OR UNTIL GOLDEN BROWN).

TOP TIP GRAB YOUR FAVORITE SAUCE AND DIP INTO THESE YUMMY BITES!

CHICKEN KIEV

INGREDIENTS

- 2 BONELESS CHICKEN BREASTS
- 4 TBSP. COOKED SPINACH
- 8 TBSP. BUTTER
- 4 TBSP. FRESH PARSLEY
- 1 EGG
- 150G | 1 CUP DRY BREADCRUMBS
- ½ TSP. PEPPER
- 1 TSP. SALT

METHOD

🍴 SERVES 2 ⏱️ 10 MINUTES PREP 🕙 10 MINUTES COOK

STEP 01 IN A BOWL, MIX BUTTER, SPINACH, PARSLEY, SALT, AND PEPPER UNTIL COMBINED.

STEP 02 SPLIT THE BUTTER MIXTURE INTO TWO SECTIONS, AND FREEZE UNTIL HARD.

STEP 03 POUND THE CHICKEN WITH A MALLET UNTIL IT BECOMES APPROX. 1.5CM | ½ IN THICK.

STEP 04 PLACE ONE SECTION OF BUTTER IN THE CENTER OF EACH CHICKEN BREAST, THEN FOLD THE CHICKEN OVER THE TOP AND WRAP TIGHTLY WITH CLING FILM. FREEZE THE CHICKEN FOR 30 MINUTES.

STEP 05 PREHEAT YOUR AIR FRYER AT 190°C | 370°F.

STEP 06 GET 2 BOWLS. IN THE 1ST BOWL, BEAT THE EGG. IN THE 2ND BOWL, ADD BREADCRUMBS.

STEP 07 COAT YOUR CHICKENS IN THE EGG, THEN COAT IN BREADCRUMBS. ADD BOTH CHICKEN BREASTS TO THE AIR FRYER AND COOK FOR 10 MINUTES, FLIPPING HALFWAY.

BAKED POTATOES

INGREDIENTS

- > 4 BAKING POTATOES
- > ½ TBSP. SUNFLOWER OIL
- > SALT AND PEPPER (TO TASTE)
- > TOPPINGS OF YOUR CHOICE

METHOD

SERVES 4 | 2 MINUTES PREP | 45 MINUTES COOK

STEP 01 WASH THE POTATOES WELL AND PAT DRY WITH KITCHEN TOWELS.

STEP 02 DRIZZLE OIL OVER THE POTATOES AND RUB INTO THE SKINS EVENLY. SEASON WITH SALT AND PEPPER (THIS WILL HELP THE SKINS BECOME CRISPY!)

STEP 03 PLACE THE POTATOES INTO THE AIR FRYER AND COOK AT 200°C | 400°F FOR 45 MINUTES.

STEP 04 CHECK ON THE POTATOES AFTER 20 MINUTES OF COOKING, AND TURN IF BECOMING TOO BROWN ON ONE SIDE.

STEP 05 ONCE COOKED – SLICE DOWN THE MIDDLE AND SERVE WITH YOUR FAVORITE TOPPINGS!

TOP TIP SOME OF THE MOST LOVED TOPPINGS ARE:
- CHEESE AND BEANS
- TUNA MAYO
- CHILI CON CARNE

HASSELBACK POTATOES

INGREDIENTS

- 2 MEDIUM GOLDEN POTATOES
- 1 TBSP. OLIVE OIL
- ½ TBSP. SEA SALT FLAKES
- ½ TBSP. PEPPER
- 3 TBSP. UNSALTED BUTTER (AT ROOM TEMPERATURE)
- 1 SPRING ONION (SCALLION, FINELY CHOPPED)

METHOD

SERVES 2

10 MINUTES PREP

30 MINUTES COOK

STEP 01
PREHEAT THE AIR FRYER TO 200°C | 400 °F.

STEP 02
USING A SHARP KNIFE, MAKE SLITS THINLY ACROSS THE POTATOES, ENSURING NOT TO CUT ALL THE WAY THROUGH (LEAVE AT LEAST 0.6CM | ¼" FROM THE BOTTOM).

STEP 03
RUB THE POTATOES WITH OIL, THEN ½ TSP. SALT, AND ½ TSP. PEPPER.

STEP 04
ADD THE POTATOES TO THE AIR FRYER, SLICED SIDE UP, AND COOK FOR 30 MINUTES UNTIL GOLDEN BROWN.

STEP 05
ADD BUTTER TO A BOWL WITH CHOPPED SCALLIONS. MIX UNTIL COMBINED, THEN BRUSH EACH POTATO WITH THE BUTTERY MIX.

SWEET CHILI CHICKEN BITES

INGREDIENTS

- 2 CHICKEN BREASTS (BONELESS)
- 1 TSP. GROUND BLACK PEPPER
- 1 TBSP. SALT
- 1 TSP. PAPRIKA
- 1 SPRING ONION (SCALLION)
- 50G | ¼ CUP ALL-PURPOSE FLOUR
- 2 EGGS
- 240G | 2 CUPS BREADCRUMBS
- 125ML | ½ CUP SWEET CHILI SAUCE
- 1 TSP. WHITE SESAME SEEDS (FOR GARNISH)

METHOD

🍴 **SERVES 2** ⏱ **10 MINUTES PREP** ⏲ **14 MINUTES COOK**

STEP 01 PAT DRY CHICKEN BREASTS WITH A PAPER TOWEL THEN SLICE INTO 2.5CM | 1" CUBES.

STEP 02 PLACE THE CHICKEN PIECES INTO A BOWL AND ADD PAPRIKA, SALT, AND PEPPER, THEN TOSS.

STEP 03 PLACE THE CHICKEN AND FLOUR INTO A FREEZER BAG, AND SHAKE WELL TO COAT ENTIRELY.

STEP 04 IN ONE BOWL, BEAT THE EGGS. IN ANOTHER BOWL, ADD BREADCRUMBS.

STEP 05 ONE PIECE AT A TIME, COAT THE CHICKEN IN THE EGG, THEN PLACE INTO THE BREADCRUMBS AND COAT WELL (USE YOUR FINGERS TO PRESS CRUMBS INTO THE CHICKEN).

STEP 06 ADD THE CHICKEN IN THE AIR FRYER AND COOK IN A SINGLE LAYER AT 190°C | 375°F FOR 12-14 MINUTES (UNTIL GOLDEN BROWN).

STEP 07 COAT THE CHICKEN THOROUGHLY IN SWEET CHILI SAUCE, THEN GARNISH WITH SCALLIONS AND SESAME SEEDS!

PIZZA BAGELS

INGREDIENTS

> 2 BAGELS
> 1 TSP. OLIVE OIL
> ¼ TSP. GARLIC POWDER
> ¼ TSP. OREGANO
> 3 TBSP. TOMATO PASTE
> 120G | ½ CUP GRATED
> MOZZARELLA

METHOD

SERVES 4 | **2 MINUTES PREP** | **07 MINUTES COOK**

STEP 01
PREHEAT THE AIR FRYER TO 190°C | 370°F.

STEP 02
CUT THE BAGELS IN HALF, AND BRUSH EACH HALF WITH OLIVE OIL, BEFORE SPRINKLING GARLIC POWDER AND OREGANO ONTO EACH HALF.

STEP 03
POP THE BAGELS INTO THE AIR FRYER FOR 3 MINUTES.

STEP 04
SPREAD EACH BAGEL SLICE WITH TOMATO PASTE AND SPRINKLE WITH MOZZARELLA.

STEP 05
PLACE EACH SLICE BACK INTO THE AIR FRYER FOR 4 MINUTES UNTIL THE CHEESE IS MELTED.

TOP TIP
WHY NOT EXPERIMENT WITH DIFFERENT PIZZA TOPPINGS LIKE PEPPERONI OR HAM AND MUSHROOM?

LAMB CHOPS

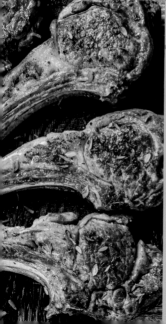

INGREDIENTS

- 8 LAMB LOIN CHOPS
- 60G | ¼ CUP BUTTER (SOFTENED)
- 1 CRUSHED GARLIC CLOVE
- 1 ½ TSP. CHOPPED ROSEMARY LEAVES

METHOD

SERVES 4 | 5 MINUTES PREP | 08 MINUTES COOK

STEP 01 PLACE BUTTER, CRUSHED GARLIC, AND ROSEMARY INTO A SMALL BOWL AND MIX WELL UNTIL COMBINED.

STEP 02 MOULD THE GARLIC BUTTER INTO A LOG SHAPE, AND PLACE INTO THE FRIDGE FOR A FEW MINUTES UNTIL FIRM.

STEP 03 PREHEAT THE AIR FRYER FOR 5 MINUTES AT 200°C | 400°F.

STEP 04 SPRAY THE CHOPS LIGHTLY WITH OIL, AND PLACE INTO THE AIR FRYER WITHOUT OVERLAPPING (YOU MIGHT NEED TO COOK THESE IN TWO BATCHES).

STEP 05 COOK THE CHOPS FOR 4 MINUTES ON EACH SIDE. CHOP THE GARLIC BUTTER INTO 8 PIECES, AND TOP EACH LAMB CHOP WITH A SLICE.

STEP 06 CLOSE THE AIR FRYER FOR 1 MINUTE UNTIL THE BUTTER HAS COMPLETELY MELTED (DON'T TURN THE AIR FRYER ON FOR THIS STEP).

TOP TIP WHY NOT TOP WITH A DRIZZLE OF MINT SAUCE TO ADD A BURST OF FLAVOR?

MEATBALLS

INGREDIENTS

- 450G | 1 LB GROUND BEEF
- 1 EGG
- 30G | ¼ CUP BREADCRUMBS
- 30G | ¼ CUP PARMESAN CHEESE
- 1 TSP. GARLIC POWDER
- 1 TSP. SALT
- 1 TSP. PEPPER
- 1 TBSP. WORCESTERSHIRE SAUCE

METHOD

 SERVES 4

 10 MINUTES PREP

 14 MINUTES COOK

STEP 01 PREHEAT THE AIR FRYER AT 190°C | 380°F.

STEP 02 CRACK THE EGG INTO A BOWL, AND MIX ALL THE OTHER LISTED INGREDIENTS TOGETHER UNTIL ENTIRELY COMBINED.

STEP 03 EQUALLY DIVIDE THE MIXTURE AND ROLL INTO BALLS.

STEP 04 PLACE INTO THE AIR FRYER WITHOUT OVERLAPPING, AND COOK FOR 12-14 MINUTES, OR UNTIL THE INSIDE IS FULLY BROWN.

TOP TIP WHY NOT ADD THE MEATBALLS TO A SUB, OR EAT ALONGSIDE SPAGHETTI?

SWEET AND SOUR CHICKEN

INGREDIENTS

- 450G | 1LB CHICKEN BREASTS, CUT INTO 4CM | 1 ½ INCH CHUNKS
- 2 TBSP. CORNSTARCH
- 250G | 1 CUP PINEAPPLE JUICE
- 125G | ½ CUP BROWN SUGAR
- 3 TBSP. RICE WINE VINEGAR
- 1 TBSP. SOY SAUCE
- ¼ TSP. GROUND GINGER
- 2 TBSP. CORNSTARCH
- 2 TBSP. WATER

METHOD

SERVES 2 | 5 MINUTES PREP | 15 MINUTES COOK

STEP 01
PREHEAT THE AIR FRYER TO 200°C | 400°F. ADD THE CHICKEN CHUNKS AND CORNSTARCH INTO A BOWL. MIX WELL UNTIL FULLY COVERED.

STEP 02
PLACE THE CHICKEN CHUNKS INTO THE AIR FRYER FOR 8-9 MINUTES, SHAKING HALFWAY, THEN REMOVE FROM THE AIR FRYER.

STEP 03
MIX TOGETHER BROWN SUGAR, PINEAPPLE JUICE, RICE WINE VINEGAR, GINGER, AND SOY SAUCE AND ADD TO THE AIR FRYER IN A TRAY THEN ALLOW TO SIMMER FOR 5 MINUTES.

STEP 04
MIX TOGETHER CORNSTARCH AND WATER IN A BOWL, THEN ADD TO THE SWEET AND SOUR SAUCE.

STEP 05
SIMMER FOR 1 MORE MINUTE, BEFORE REMOVING THE DRAWER AND ADDING THE CHICKEN, COATING WELL WITH THE SAUCE.

TOP TIP
WE SUGGEST SERVING WITH BOILED RICE AND A DASH OF SOY SAUCE!

BEEF AND BROCCOLI

INGREDIENTS

- 450G | 1 LB STEAK (SLICED INTO STRIPS)
- 2 CLOVES OF GARLIC (GRATED)
- 2 TSP. PEELED FRESH GINGER (GRATED)
- 350G | 12 OZ. SMALL BROCCOLI FLORETS
- 120ML | ½ CUP. LIGHT SOY SAUCE
- 60ML | ¼ CUP WATER
- 1 TBSP. CORNSTARCH
- 2 TBSP. BROWN SUGAR
- 1 TSP. TOASTED SESAME OIL

METHOD

SERVES 10 | 8 MINUTES PREP | 10 MINUTES COOK

SAUCE:

STEP 01 IN A MICROWAVABLE BOWL, ADD WATER, BROWN SUGAR, SOY SAUCE, AND CORNSTARCH. MICROWAVE FOR APPROX. 2 MINUTES, STIRRING HALFWAY UNTIL THICKENED. ADD OIL AND SPRINKLE WITH BLACK PEPPER, BEFORE STIRRING.

BROCCOLI AND STEAK:

STEP 01 IN ANOTHER BOWL, ADD STEAK, 3 TBSP. OF YOUR SAUCE, GARLIC, AND GINGER. TOSS THE STEAK AROUND THEN ALLOW TO SIT FOR 5 MINUTES.

STEP 02 ADD OIL AND BROCCOLI, AND MIX TO COMBINE.

STEP 03 PLACE THE STEAK AND BROCCOLI MIXTURE INTO THE AIR FRYER IN A SINGLE LAYER (YOU MAY NEED TO COOK IN TWO BATCHES), AND COOK FOR 8-10 MINUTES AT 200°C|400°F.

STEP 04 ADD THE STEAK AND BROCCOLI INTO THE REMAINING SAUCE, THEN GENTLY MIX UNTIL COATED.

TOP TIP WHY NOT SERVE THIS DISH WITH YOUR FAVORITE RICE?

BLACK BEAN FRITTERS

INGREDIENTS

- 1 CAN OF BLACK BEANS
- 4 OZ. MUSHROOMS
- 125G | ½ SMALL BROWN ONION (FINELY CHOPPED)
- 125G | ½ CUP BREADCRUMBS
- 2 TBSP. WHITE MISO
- ½ TSP. GARLIC POWDER
- 3 TBSP. TAHINI
- ½ TSP. SALT
- ½ TSP. SMOKED PAPRIKA
- 2 TBSP. FRESH DILL (FINELY CHOPPED)
- 2 TBSP. WATER
- 2 TBSP. WHITE WINE VINEGAR
- SLICED CHERRY TOMATOES AND CUCUMBERS (FOR GARNISH)

METHOD

SERVES 4 · 10 MINUTES PREP · 15 MINUTES COOK

STEP 01
IN A BOWL, ADD BEANS, ONION, BREADCRUMBS, MUSHROOMS, MISO, GARLIC POWDER, PAPRIKA, 1 TBSP. TAHINI, AND ¼ TSP. SALT.

STEP 02
MASH TOGETHER UNTIL COMBINED. FORM INTO 8 PATTIES (AROUND 2 ½ INCH | 6CM THICK)

STEP 03
LIGHTLY SPRAY THE AIR FRYER WITH OIL, AND ADD THE PATTIES INTO THE DRAWER (YOU MAY NEED TO COOK IN TWO BATCHES).

STEP 04
GIVE THE PATTIES A LIGHT SPRAY OF OIL THEN COOK AT 200°C | 400°F FOR 15 MINUTES, FLIPPING HALFWAY.

STEP 05
IN A BOWL ADD DILL, VINEGAR, WATER, TAHINI, AND ¼ TSP. SALT AND WHISK WELL UNTIL SMOOTH (THE MIXTURE SHOULD BE RUNNY, ADD MORE WATER IF TOO THICK).

STEP 06
DRIZZLE THE BEAN FRITTERS WITH THE DRESSING, AND SERVE!

SMASHED AVOCADO TOAST

INGREDIENTS

- 2 SLICES BREAD (WHOLE WHEAT OR SOURDOUGH WORKS BEST)
- 1 LARGE AVOCADO
- 2 LARGE EGGS
- 1 TBSP. FRESH LEMON JUICE
- 2 TSP. CHOPPED FRESH BASIL LEAVES
- SALT
- 4 TSP. LUKEWARM WATER

METHOD

STEP 01
PLACE BOTH SLICES OF BREAD IN TO THE AIR FRYER IN A SINGLE LAYER AND COOK FOR 3-4 MINUTES AT 180°C | 350°F, FLIPPING HALFWAY.

STEP 02
SCOOP THE FLESH OF THE AVOCADO INTO A BOWL AND ADD BASIL, LEMON JUICE, AND A PINCH OF SALT. MASH WITH A FORK UNTIL THE MIXTURE IS CHUNKY BUT MIXED WELL.

STEP 03
LIGHTLY SPRAY 2 RAMEKINS WITH OLIVE OIL, AND ADD 2 TSP. WATER INTO EACH.

STEP 04
CRACK AN EGG INTO EACH OF THE RAMEKINS AND COOK IN THE AIR FRYER AT 180°C | 350°F, FOR 6-8 MINUTES (SO THE WHITES ARE HARDENED BUT THE YOLKS ARE STILL RUNNY).

STEP 05
SPREAD THE AVOCADO MIX OVER EACH SLICE OF TOAST, AND REMOVE THE EGGS FROM THE RAMEKIN, PLACING THE EGGS UPSIDE DOWN ON TOP OF THE TOAST.

TOP TIP
WHY NOT GARNISH WITH SOME CHERRY TOMATOES AND BASIL?

CHICKEN TIKKA WRAPS

INGREDIENTS

- 2 CHICKEN BREASTS (DICED)
- 120ML | 1/2 CUP PLAIN YOGURT
- 2 TBSP. TIKKA MASALA PASTE
- 1 TSP. GROUND CUMIN
- 1 TSP. PAPRIKA
- 2 TORTILLA WRAPS
- SHREDDED LETTUCE
- HANDFUL OF MINT LEAVES
- MANGO CHUTNEY
- 1/2 RED ONION (SLICED)
- SALT AND PEPPER (TO TASTE)

METHOD

SERVES 2 | 10 MINUTES PREP | 15 MINUTES COOK

STEP 01 SLICE YOUR CHICKEN BREASTS INTO BITE SIZE PIECES.

STEP 02 COMBINE THE YOGURT, TIKKA PASTE, CUMIN, AND PAPRIKA, AND ADD SALT AND PEPPER TO TASTE.

STEP 03 COAT YOUR CHICKEN WITH THE YOGURT MIXTURE AND MARINATE FOR AT LEAST 30 MINUTES.

STEP 04 PREHEAT YOUR AIR FRYER TO 180°C | 360°F.

STEP 05 ADD YOUR CHICKEN AND COOK FOR 12-15 MINUTES, TURNING HALFWAY.

STEP 06 BUILD YOUR WRAPS WITH MANGO CHUTNEY, ANY REMAINING PLAIN YOGURT, MINT LEAVES, AND SLICED RED ONION, AND ENJOY!

GRILLED CHEESE

INGREDIENTS

- 2 SLICES SOURDOUGH BREAD
- 4 SLICES CHEDDAR (OR YOUR FAVORITE CHEESE) - CUT ENOUGH TO FILL THE BREAD!
- 1 TBSP. BUTTER (OR MARGARINE IF PREFERRED)

METHOD

 SERVES 1

 2 MINUTES PREP

 10 MINUTES COOK

STEP 01 PREHEAT THE AIR FRYER AT 180°C | 350°F.

STEP 02 SPREAD BUTTER OVER ONE SIDE OF BOTH SLICES OF BREAD.

STEP 03 TURN ONE SLICE OVER (UNBUTTERED SLICE NOW FACING UP), AND ARRANGE THE CHEESE EVENLY.

STEP 04 PLACE THE SECOND SLICE OF BREAD (BUTTER SIDE UP) ON TOP OF THE CHEESE.

STEP 05 PLACE THE SANDWICH INTO THE AIR FRYER AND COOK FOR 10 MINUTES, FLIPPING HALFWAY.

CHICKEN WINGS

INGREDIENTS

- 16 CHICKEN WINGS
- 1 TSP. SHAOXING RICE WINE
- 3 TBSP. PLAIN FLOUR
- 1 TSP. SESAME OIL
- ½ TSP. WHITE PEPPER
- ¼ TSP. GROUND GINGER
- 1 RED CHILI
  (THINLY SLICED)
- 2-3 CLOVES OF GARLIC
  (CHOPPED)
- 2 SPRING ONIONS
  (SCALLIONS, THINLY SLICED)

METHOD

STEP 01 PREHEAT THE AIR FRYER TO 180°C | 350°F.

STEP 02 IN A BOWL, ADD THE CHICKEN WINGS THEN ADD RICE WINE AND SESAME OIL. SPRINKLE FLOUR, GINGER, WHITE PEPPER, AND A DASH OF SALT AND BLACK PEPPER OVER THE TOP, THEN MIX AROUND, ENSURING THE CHICKEN IS EVENLY COATED.

STEP 03 LIGHTLY SPRAY THE AIR FRYER WITH OIL AND LAY OUT THE CHICKEN IN A SINGLE LAYER (YOU MIGHT NEED TO COOK IN TWO BATCHES).

STEP 04 LIGHTLY SPRAY THE CHICKEN WITH OIL THEN COOK FOR 10 MINUTES.

STEP 05 PLACE CHILI, SCALLIONS, AND GARLIC INTO A BOWL AND ADD THE CHICKEN. SHAKE THE BOWL TO COAT THE CHICKEN WINGS.

STEP 06 ADD EVERYTHING BACK INTO THE AIR FRYER AND COOK FOR 10-15 MINUTES (UNTIL COOKED THROUGH).

THAI SWEET CHILI SALMON BITES

INGREDIENTS

- › 2 SALMON FILLETS (SKINLESS)
- › 60ML | 1/4 CUP SWEET CHILI SAUCE
- › 2 TBSP. SOY SAUCE
- › 1 TSP. LIME JUICE
- › 2 GARLIC CLOVES (MINCED)
- › 1 TSP. GINGER (GRATED)
- › 1 TBSP. FRESH CORIANDER (CILANTRO)

METHOD

SERVES 2 | 10 MINUTES PREP | 10 MINUTES COOK

STEP 01 CUT THE SALMON FILLETS INTO BITE-SIZED PIECES.

STEP 02 COMBINE THE SWEET CHILI, SOY SAUCE, LIME JUICE, GARLIC, AND GINGER, AND COAT YOUR SALMON. MARINATE FOR AT LEAST 30 MINUTES.

STEP 03 PREHEAT THE AIR FRYER TO 180°C | 350°F.

STEP 04 DRIZZLE THE MARINATED SALMON WITH A NEUTRAL OIL AND PLACE INTO THE AIR FRYER.

STEP 05 COOK FOR 8-10 MINUTES, TURNING HALFWAY AND ADDING MORE MARINADE.

STEP 06 REMOVE AND GARNISH WITH CHOPPED CILANTRO.

GREEK SALMON

INGREDIENTS

- 450G | 1 LB SALMON
- 3 TBSP. OLIVE OIL
- 1 TBSP. LEMON JUICE (FRESHLY SQUEEZED)
- 1 TBSP. FRESH DILL (CHOPPED)
- 1 TSP. DRIED OREGANO
- 1 CRUSHED GARLIC CLOVE
- ½ TSP. SALT
- ½ TSP. GROUND BLACK PEPPER

METHOD

 SERVES 3

 5 MINUTES PREP

10 MINUTES COOK

STEP 01
REHEAT THE AIR FRYER TO 200°C | 400°F. SLICE THE SALMON INTO FILLETS, AND USING A KITCHEN TOWEL, PAT THE PIECES DRY.

STEP 02
IN A BOWL, ADD LEMON JUICE, OLIVE OIL, OREGANO, GARLIC, DILL, SALT, AND PEPPER, AND MIX THOROUGHLY.

STEP 03
POUR THE MIXTURE OVER THE SALMON AND ALLOW TO SIT FOR A MINUTE.

STEP 04
PLACE THE SALMON INTO THE AIR FRYER AND COOK FOR 10 MINUTES THEN PLATE UP AND SERVE.

TOP TIP
WE LIKE TO SERVE OURS WITH LONG GRAIN RICE!

GOAT'S CHEESE SLICES

INGREDIENTS

> 1 READY-MADE SHEET
> OF PUFF PASTRY
> (35X23CM | 14X9IN.)
> 4 TBSP. PESTO
> 4 CHERRY TOMATOES
> 4 TBSP. GOAT'S CHEESE
> 2 TSP. MILK
> (TO BRUSH PASTRY)

METHOD

SERVES 2 | 5 MINUTES PREP | 06 MINUTES COOK

STEP 01 PREHEAT THE AIR FRYER TO 180°C | 350°F.

STEP 02 CUT THE PASTRY SHEET IN HALF AND FOLD IN THE EDGES OF EACH SLICE TO MAKE A CRUST (SO YOUR TOPPINGS DON'T LEAK OUT).

STEP 03 PRICK A FEW HOLES INTO THE BASE OF EACH SLICE USING A FORK.

STEP 04 ADD THE TOPPINGS OVER EACH SLICE, CUTTING THE TOMATOES IN HALF BEFORE ADDING WITH THE PESTO AND GOAT'S CHEESE.

STEP 05 BRUSH THE PASTRY EDGES WITH MILK, THIS WILL HELP THE CRUST BECOME DARKER DURING COOKING.

STEP 06 ADD TO YOUR AIR FRYER AND COOK FOR 6 MINUTES (YOU MAY NEED TO COOK THESE SEPARATELY DEPENDING ON THE SIZE OF YOUR AIR FRYER).

STEP 07 FOR A RICHER DEPTH OF FLAVOR YOU COULD ROAST YOUR TOMATOES WITH A DRIZZLE OF OLIVE OIL AND GARLIC IN YOUR AIR FRYER BEFORE ADDING TO THE SLICE!

BUFFALO CAULIFLOWER BITES

INGREDIENTS

- 500G | 4 CUPS CAULIFLOWER FLORETS
- 2 TBSP. BUTTER
- 1 TBSP. OLIVE OIL
- 125G | ½ CUP CAYENNE PEPPER HOT SAUCE (OR YOUR FAVORITE HOT SAUCE)
- 125G | ½ CUP ALL-PURPOSE FLOUR
- 3 TBSP. DRIED PARSLEY
- 125G | ½ TBSP. GARLIC POWDER
- 1 TSP. SALT

METHOD

SERVES 4 | 10 MINUTES PREP | 15 MINUTES COOK

STEP 01 MELT THE BUTTER AND ADD HOT SAUCE AND OLIVE OIL BEFORE MIXING WELL.

STEP 02 PLACE THE CAULIFLOWER FLORETS INTO A BOWL AND POUR YOUR MIXTURE OVER THE TOP. STIR GENTLY UNTIL ALL THE CAULIFLOWER IS COATED.

STEP 03 IN ANOTHER BOWL, ADD FLOUR, GARLIC POWDER, PARSLEY, AND SEASONING, AND MIX WELL.

STEP 04 SPRINKLE A HANDFUL OF THE MIXTURE ONTO THE CAULIFLOWER AND MIX UNTIL COATED AGAIN.

STEP 05 PLACE THE CAULIFLOWER INTO THE AIR FRYER, WITHOUT OVERCROWDING (YOU CAN COOK IN TWO BATCHES IF NEEDED).

STEP 06 AIR FRY FOR 15 MINUTES AT 180°C | 350°F, SHAKING THE DRAWER OFTEN.

TOP TIP WE LIKE TO EAT OURS WITH A SIDE OF RANCH DRESSING!

CRISPY BROCCOLI WITH ALMONDS

INGREDIENTS

- 1 LARGE HEAD OF BROCCOLI
- 30G | 1/4 CUP SLICED ALMONDS
- 2 TBSP. OLIVE OIL
- 2 GARLIC CLOVES (MINCED)
- ZEST OF 1 LEMON
- 1/2 TSP. CHILI FLAKES
- SALT AND PEPPER (TO TASTE)

METHOD

SERVES 4 | 5 MINUTES PREP | 10 MINUTES COOK

STEP 01 CUT YOUR BROCCOLI INTO FLORETS.

STEP 02 IN A LARGE BOWL, COAT YOUR BROCCOLI WITH OLIVE OIL, GARLIC, LEMON ZEST, CHILI FLAKES, SALT, AND PEPPER.

STEP 03 PREHEAT YOUR AIR FRYER TO 200°C | 390°F FOR ABOUT 3-5 MINUTES.

STEP 04 PLACE THE BROCCOLI INTO THE AIR FRYER AND COOK FOR 6-8 MINUTES, SHAKING HALFWAY.

STEP 05 ADD THE ALMONDS AND COOK FOR A FURTHER 2-3 MINUTES.

STEP 06 PLATE UP AND SERVE.

TOP TIP WE LOVE TO TOP WITH FRESH CHERRY TOMATOES, AND ADD SOME CRISPY FRIED CHICKEN FOR EXTRA PROTIEN.

GARLIC GREEN BEANS

INGREDIENTS

- ➤ 450G | 1 LB GREEN BEANS (ENDS TRIMMED, CUT INTO 3 INCH SEGMENTS)
- ➤ 8 PEELED GARLIC CLOVES
- ➤ 2 TBSP. CORNSTARCH
- ➤ 1 TBSP. OLIVE OIL
- ➤ 1 TBSP. SOY SAUCE
- ➤ ½ TSP. GRATED FRESH GINGER
- ➤ ¼ TSP. GROUND WHITE PEPPER
- ➤ ½ TSP. SALT
- ➤ ½ TSP. FRESHLY GROUND BLACK PEPPER

METHOD

SERVES 4 | 10 MINUTES PREP | 12 MINUTES COOK

STEP 01 TRIM THE ENDS OF THE GREEN BEANS AND SLICE INTO SEGMENTS.

STEP 02 IN A BOWL, ADD GREEN BEANS THEN ADD GARLIC, OIL, SOY SAUCE, CORNSTARCH, GINGER, WHITE AND BLACK PEPPER, AND SALT.

STEP 03 MIX UNTIL ALL THE GREEN BEANS ARE EVENLY COATED.

STEP 04 ADD THE GREEN BEAN MIXTURE INTO THE AIR FRYER AND COOK AT 200°C | 400°F FOR 10-12 MINUTES (OR UNTIL CRISPY AND GOLDEN).

CRISPY RAVIOLI BITES

INGREDIENTS

- 250G | 9 OZ FRESH RAVIOLI (CAN ALSO USE ANY STUFFED PASTA OF YOUR CHOICE!)
- 3 TBSP. OLIVE OIL
- 1.5 TSP. ITALIAN SEASONING
- 1 TSP. GARLIC POWDER
- 3 TBSP. GRATED PARMESAN
- ½ TSP. SALT
- ½ TSP. PEPPER

METHOD

STEP 01
COOK YOUR RAVIOLI AS PER THE PACKET INSTRUCTIONS.

STEP 02
ONCE THE RAVIOLI IS COOKED, PLACE ONTO A PAPER TOWEL TO DRY.

STEP 03
WITH THE RAVIOLI DRY, PLACE INTO A BOWL AND TOSS WITH ALL OTHER INGREDIENTS, ENSURING EACH PIECE IS COATED.

STEP 04
PLACE THE COATED RAVIOLI INTO AN AIR FRYER AT 180°C | 350°F - THIS MAY NEED TO BE DONE IN BATCHES TO PREVENT OVERCROWDING!

STEP 05
COOK FOR 5 MINUTES, OR UNTIL CRISPY AND BROWNED.

TOP TIP
SERVE WITH YOUR FAVORITE MARINARA DIP, AND SPRINKLE WITH SOME MORE GRATED PARMESAN!

CHEESE BITES

INGREDIENTS

- BLOCK OF MOZZARELLA (OR YOUR CHEESE OF CHOICE) CUT INTO BITE-SIZED PIECES
- 30G | ¼ CUP FLOUR
- 2 LARGE EGGS
- 150G | 1 CUP DRY BREADCRUMBS
- 1 TSP. HERBS (OF YOUR CHOICE)
- 1 TSP. SALT
- 2 TSP. WATER

METHOD

SERVES 4 | 5 MINUTES PREP | 08 MINUTES COOK

STEP 01 SLICE EACH MOZZARELLA STICK INTO BITE-SIZED PIECES.

STEP 02 TAKE 3 BOWLS. PLACE FLOUR INTO THE 1ST BOWL.

STEP 03 IN THE 2ND BOWL, WHISK BOTH EGGS AND 2 TEASPOONS OF WATER TOGETHER.

STEP 04 IN A 3RD BOWL, ADD BREADCRUMBS, SALT, AND HERBS (WE SUGGEST BASIL, THYME, OR OREGANO), AND STIR WELL.

STEP 05 DIP THE CHEESE FULLY INTO THE 1ST BOWL, THEN INTO THE 2ND BOWL. NOW ROLL THE CHEESE IN THE 3RD BOWL, COATING ENTIRELY.

STEP 06 REPEAT FOR ALL THE CHEESE BLOCKS, THEN COOK IN THE AIR FRYER AT 180°C | 350°F FOR 8 MINUTES (OR UNTIL GOLDEN).

TOP TIP WE LOVE TO DIP OUR CHEESE BITES INTO BBQ OR MARINARA SAUCE!

SPRING ROLLS

INGREDIENTS

> 1 TBSP. OIL
> 1 TSP. GROUND GINGER
> 450G | 1 LB GROUND MEAT (OR MUSHROOMS!)
> 1 TSP. ONION POWDER
> ½ TSP. BLACK PEPPER
> 1 TBSP. RICE VINEGAR
> 1 TBSP. SOY SAUCE
> 2 CRUSHED GARLIC CLOVES
> 2 SPRING ONIONS (SCALLIONS)
> 75G | 1 ½ CUPS SHREDDED CABBAGE
> 8 SPRING ROLL WRAPPERS

METHOD

STEP 01
IN A SAUCEPAN, HEAT THE OIL ON MEDIUM-HIGH HEAT, THEN ADD THE MEAT AND COOK UNTIL BROWNED.

STEP 02
ADD ONION POWDER, GINGER, VINEGAR, GARLIC, SOY SAUCE, SPRING ONIONS, AND PEPPER INTO THE SAUCEPAN AND COOK UNTIL MOST OF THE JUICE EVAPORATES.

STEP 03
ADD CABBAGE AND COOK FOR 2 MORE MINUTES. DIAGONALLY LAY A SPRING ROLL WRAPPER, AND PLACE 2-3 SPOONFULS OF THE MEAT MIXTURE IN THE CENTER.

STEP 04
DAMPEN THE EDGE OF THE WRAPPER AND FOLD BOTH SIDES TO THE CENTER.

STEP 05
FOLD THE BOTTOM CORNER UP AND ROLL OVER THE FILLING TIGHTLY. DAMPEN THE LAST CORNER, AND SEAL IT DOWN.

STEP 06
LIGHTLY SPRAY THE SPRING ROLLS AND THE AIR FRYER DRAWER WITH OIL, THEN COOK FOR 8 MINUTES AT 190°C | 380°F, FLIPPING HALFWAY.

CHEESY GARLIC BREAD

INGREDIENTS

- 10 SLICES OF A BAGUETTE
- 1 TBSP. UNSALTED BUTTER
- 2 TBSP. CREAM CHEESE
- 1 TSP. DRY PARSLEY FLAKES
- 1 TSP. DRY OREGANO
- 1 TSP. GROUND GARLIC
- ½ TSP. BLACK PEPPER
- PINCH OF SALT
- 225G | 1 CUP GRATED MOZZARELLA
- 1 CLOVE GARLIC (MINCED)

METHOD

SERVES 10 | 5 MINUTES PREP | 08 MINUTES COOK

STEP 01 ADD BUTTER, CREAM CHEESE, PARSLEY, MINCED AND GROUND GARLIC, OREGANO, SALT, AND PEPPER INTO A BOWL AND MIX WELL.

STEP 02 SLICE THE BAGUETTE INTO 10 SLICES, THEN SPREAD THE GARLIC BUTTER EVENLY ON ONE SIDE OF EACH SLICE.

STEP 03 PLACE THE GARLIC BREAD INTO THE AIR FRYER, ENSURING NOT TO OVERLAP, AT 190°C | 370°F.

STEP 04 COOK FOR 4-5 MINUTES, UNTIL CRISPY ROUND THE EDGES AND GOLDEN IN COLOR.

STEP 05 SPRINKLE MOZZARELLA OVER EACH SLICE OF BREAD, THEN AIR FRY FOR ANOTHER 2-3 MINUTES UNTIL THE CHEESE HAS MELTED.

TOP TIP TO MAKE THIS ALREADY DELICIOUS DISH EVEN BETTER, WHY NOT GARNISH WITH FRESH PARSLEY?

DIRTY FRIES

INGREDIENTS

- 2 POTATOES (RUSSET ARE BEST!)
- 2-3 TSP. OLIVE OIL
- ½ TSP. SALT
- 1 TSP. BLACK PEPPER
- ⅓ TSP. FRIES SEASONING
- 120G | 1 CUP CHEESE (SHREDDED)
- 4 SLICES BACON (COOKED)
- ¼ CUP SPRING ONIONS (SCALLIONS, SLICED)

METHOD

STEP 01 PREHEAT AIR FRYER TO 195°C | 380°F.

STEP 02 SLICE POTATOES INTO SMALL FRIES.

STEP 03 SUBMERGE SLICED FRIES INTO A BOWL OF COLD WATER TO SOAK.

STEP 04 DRAIN THE FRIES AND PAT DRY WITH A PAPER TOWEL.

STEP 05 ADD TO A BOWL WITH OIL, SALT, AND PEPPER AND TOSS TO COAT.

STEP 06 PLACE FRIES INTO THE AIR FRYER AND COOK FOR 10-15 MINUTES, SHAKING THE DRAWER OCCASIONALLY.

STEP 07 SPRINKLE THE SEASONING OVER THE FRIES, THEN FOLLOW WITH CHEDDAR AND BACON. COOK AGAIN FOR 2 MINUTES (OR UNTIL CHEESE IS MELTED).

STEP 08 REMOVE FROM THE AIR FRYER AND SPRINKLE SCALLIONS ON TOP!

ROAST POTATOES

INGREDIENTS

- 650G|1 ½ LB POTATOES
- 2 TBSP. OLIVE OIL
- 1 TSP. SALT
- ½ TSP. SMOKED PAPRIKA
- ½ TSP. GARLIC POWDER
- ¼ TSP. GROUND BLACK PEPPER

METHOD

STEP 01 PREHEAT THE AIR FRYER AT 195°C | 380°F.

STEP 02 SLICE THE POTATOES INTO HALVES OR QUARTERS (OR APPROX. 1 INCH PIECES).

STEP 03 IN A BOWL, ADD THE POTATOES ALONG WITH OLIVE OIL, GARLIC POWDER, PAPRIKA, SALT, AND PEPPER.

STEP 04 ROLL THE POTATOES AROUND IN THE BOWL TO ENSURE THEY'RE COATED EVENLY.

STEP 05 PLACE POTATOES INTO THE AIR FRYER AND COOK FOR 10 MINUTES.

STEP 06 FLIP THE POTATOES AND COOK FOR ANOTHER 10 MINUTES.

GARLIC AND HERB CROUTONS

INGREDIENTS

> - 4 THICK SLICES OF WHITE BREAD
> - 1 TSP. PARSLEY FLAKES
> - ½ TSP. GARLIC POWDER
> - ½ TSP. SEASONED SALT
> - 3 TBSP. UNSALTED BUTTER (MELTED)

METHOD

SERVES 6 | **5 MINUTES PREP** | **06 MINUTES COOK**

STEP 01 PREHEAT THE AIR FRYER TO 200°C | 400°F.

STEP 02 IN A BOWL, WHISK GARLIC POWDER, PARSLEY, SEASONED SALT, AND BUTTER TOGETHER.

STEP 03 SLICE THE BREAD INTO CUBES AND ADD TO THE BOWL THEN TOSS UNTIL EVENLY COATED.

STEP 04 ADD THE CROUTONS TO THE AIR FRYER AND COOK FOR 6 MINUTES, SHAKING THE DRAWER HALFWAY THROUGH.

GARLIC PARMESAN SWEET POTATO BITES

INGREDIENTS

- 2 SWEET POTATOES (PEELED AND DICED)
- 2 TBSP. OLIVE OIL
- 2 GARLIC CLOVES (MINCED)
- 30G | 1/3 CUP PARMESAN (GRATED)
- 1 TSP. GARLIC POWDER
- 1 TSP. DRIED PARSLEY
- 1/2 TSP. PAPRIKA
- SALT AND PEPPER (TO TASTE)

METHOD

SERVES 4   5 MINUTES PREP | 15 MINUTES COOK

STEP 01 PREHEAT YOUR AIR FRYER TO 200°C | 400°F.

STEP 02 IN A LARGE BOWL, COMBINE YOUR POTATO CUBES, OLIVE OIL, MINCED GARLIC, PARMESAN, GARLIC POWDER, DRIED PARSLEY, PAPRIKA, SALT, AND PEPPER, AND COAT EVENLY.

STEP 03 PLACE INTO YOUR AIR FRYER AND COOK FOR 12-15 MINUTES, OR UNTIL CRISPY AND GOLDEN, SHAKING HALFWAY.

STEP 04 GARNISH WITH MORE PARMESAN AND SOME BLACK PEPPER.

ONION BHAJIS

INGREDIENTS

- 2 BROWN ONIONS
- 4 TBSP. RICE FLOUR
- 1 RED ONION
- 1 TSP. SEA SALT
- 1 TSP. GARLIC PASTE
- 1 TSP. SLICED GINGER
- 3 GREEN CHILIES (CHOPPED FINELY)
- ½ TSP. CUMIN
- ½ TSP. TURMERIC
- 1 TSP. KASHMIRI CHILI POWDER (OPTIONAL)
- 125G | 1 CUP SIFTED GRAM FLOUR
- HANDFUL OF CHOPPED CORIANDER LEAVES (CILANTRO)

METHOD

SERVES 4 | 10 MINUTES PREP | 15 MINUTES COOK

STEP 01 FINELY SLICE THE ONIONS. MIX WITH SALT AND SET ASIDE FOR MINIMUM 1 HOUR BEFORE COOKING.

STEP 02 REMOVE ONIONS AND SQUEEZE THE ONIONS TO RELEASE WATER.

STEP 03 ADD ALL OF THE REMAINING INGREDIENTS TO THE ONIONS AND MIX WELL.

STEP 04 DIVIDE THE MIXTURE INTO SMALL BHAJIS AND PLACE IN THE BASKET (YOU MAY NEED TO COOK THESE IN BATCHES DEPENDING ON THE SIZE OF YOUR AIR FRYER).

STEP 05 PREHEAT THE AIR FRYER FOR 5 MINUTES AT 176°C | 380°F.

STEP 06 COOK THE BHAJIS FOR 15 MINUTES UNTIL CRISPY.

DEVILED EGGS

INGREDIENTS

- 6 EGGS
- 3 TBSP. MAYONNAISE
- 3 TBSP. RELISH
  (USE A RELISH OF YOUR
  CHOICE! SWEET RELISH
  WORKS WELL)
- 1 TSP. SALT
- ½ TSP. PEPPER
- PAPRIKA (FOR DUSTING)

METHOD

STEP 01 PLACE EACH EGG INTO THE AIR FRYER AND COOK FOR 15-17 MINUTES AT 120°C | 250°F.

STEP 02 TAKE THE EGGS OUT OF THE AIR FRYER AND PLACE DIRECTLY INTO A BOWL OF ICE WATER, ALLOWING THEM TO SIT FOR 5-10 MINUTES.

STEP 03 PEEL THE EGGS, AND SLICE IN HALF LENGTHWAYS. SCOOP OUT THE YOLK FROM EACH EGG AND PLACE INTO A BOWL. USE A FORK TO BREAK THE YOLK UP AND MAKE FLUFFY.

STEP 04 ADD RELISH, MAYONAISE, SALT, AND PEPPER TO THE YOLKS AND MIX WELL.

STEP 05 EQUALLY PLACE THE YOLK MIX BACK INTO THE EGG WHITES, THEN SPRINKLE WITH A LITTLE BIT OF PAPRIKA!

JALAPEÑO POPPERS

INGREDIENTS

- 5 FRESH JALAPEÑOS
- 115G | 4OZ CREAM CHEESE
- 60G | ½ CUP SHREDDED CHEDDAR CHEESE
- 2 CHOPPED SPRING ONIONS (SCALLIONS)
- ½ TSP. GARLIC POWDER
- ½ TSP. BLACK PEPPER
- ¼ TSP. SALT
- 1 TBSP. BUTTER
- 15G | ¼ CUP PANKO BREADCRUMBS

METHOD

SERVES **10**

10 MINUTES PREP

08 MINUTES COOK

STEP 01
CAREFULLY SLICE THE JALAPEÑOS LENGTHWISE IN HALF, AND HOLLOW THEM OUT, REMOVING THE SEEDS.

STEP 02
IN A BOWL, ADD CHEDDAR CHEESE, CREAM CHEESE, SCALLIONS, GARLIC POWDER, SALT, AND PEPPER AND MIX WELL.

STEP 03
SPOON THE MIXTURE EVENLY INTO EACH JALAPEÑO. ADD BREADCRUMBS AND MELTED BUTTER INTO A SMALL BOWL AND MIX.

STEP 04
DIP THE CHEESE FILLING SIDE OF THE JALAPEÑOS INTO THE BREADCRUMBS, AND LAY CHEESE SIDE UP IN THE AIR FRYER.

STEP 05
COOK FOR 5-8 MINUTES AT 190°C | 375°F.

TOP TIP
WHY NOT GET SOME SOUR CREAM DIP TO COMPLEMENT THE TASTE?

HASH BROWNS

INGREDIENTS

- 425G | 3 CUPS POTATOES (PEELED AND GRATED - RUSSET POTATOES WORK BEST!)
- 65ML | ¼ CUP WATER
- 1 TBSP. VEGETABLE OIL
- ⅓ TSP. SALT

METHOD

SERVES 4 | **5 MINUTES PREP** | **20 MINUTES COOK**

STEP 01
PREHEAT THE AIR FRYER TO 200°C | 400°F.

STEP 02
IN A MICROWAVABLE BOWL, ADD GRATED POTATOES AND WATER AND TOSS UNTIL THE POTATO IS ENTIRELY COATED.

STEP 03
COVER WITH PLASTIC WRAP AND PIERCE WITH A FORK, THEN ADD TO THE MICROWAVE AND COOK FOR 3 ½ TO 4 MINUTES, STOPPING TO SHAKE THE POTATOES EACH MINUTE.

STEP 04
ALLOW THE POTATOES TO COOL THEN ADD OIL AND SALT AND TOSS AGAIN. FORM 6 RECTANGLES WITH THE POTATOES, THEN ADD TO THE AIR FRYER.

STEP 05
COOK FOR 15-20 MINUTES UNTIL CRISPY AND GOLDEN BROWN!

TOP TIP
WHY NOT DIP THESE DELICIOUS BITES INTO YOUR FAVORITE SAUCE?

FRIED PICKLES

INGREDIENTS

- ❯ 300G | 2 CUPS DILL PICKLE SLICES (CAN ALSO SLICE YOUR OWN PICKLES)
- ❯ 75G | ½ CUP PLAIN BREADCRUMBS
- ❯ 25G | ¼ CUP FINELY GRATED PARMESAN
- ❯ 1 TSP. DRIED OREGANO
- ❯ 1 TSP. GARLIC POWDER
- ❯ 1 LARGE EGG
- ❯ RANCH DRESSING FOR SERVING (SOUR CREAM DIP ALSO WORKS WELL!)

METHOD

 SERVES 3

 10 MINUTES PREP

 10 MINUTES COOK

STEP 01 USING PAPER TOWELS, PAT THE PICKLE SLICES DRY.

STEP 02 IN A BOWL, ADD BREADCRUMBS, OREGANO, GARLIC POWDER, AND PARMESAN, AND STIR.

STEP 03 IN ANOTHER BOWL, WHISK 1 TBSP. OF WATER WITH AN EGG.

STEP 04 COMPLETELY DIP EACH PICKLE SLICE IN EGG, THEN INTO THE BREADCRUMB MIXTURE.

STEP 05 ADD THE PICKLES TO THE AIR FRYER IN A SINGLE LAYER, THEN COOK FOR 10 MINUTES AT 200°C | 400°F.

TOP TIP WE FIND RANCH DRESSING IS THE PERFECT COMBINATION!

HALLOUMI FRIES

INGREDIENTS

- 2 BLOCKS HALLOUMI
- 2 TBSP. PLAIN FLOUR
- 1/2 TSP. DRIED OREGANO
- 1/2 TSP. GARLIC POWDER
- 1/2 TSP. SMOKED PAPRIKA
- 1/2 TSP. CRACKED BLACK PEPPER

METHOD

SERVES
2

10
MINUTES PREP

15
MINUTES
COOK

STEP 01
SLICE THE HALLOUMI BLOCKS IN HALF LENGTHWAYS, AND THEN SLICE EACH HALF INTO CHUNKY STRIPS TO FORM YOUR FRIES.

STEP 02
COMBINE ALL OF THE DRIED INGREDIENTS IN A SEPARATE BOWL.

STEP 03
GENTLY TOSS YOUR HALLOUMI INTO YOUR SEASONED FLOUR MIXTURE, ENSURING THEY ARE WELL COATED!

STEP 04
PLACE THE HALLOUMI IN A SINGLE LAYER INTO YOUR AIR FRYER AND COOK AT 180°C | 350°F FOR 12-15 MINUTES, OR UNTIL GOLDEN BROWN.

TOP TIP
YOU MAY NEED TO DO THESE IN BATCHES! SERVE WITH DIPPING SAUCE. TOMATO DIPPING SAUCE IS A GREAT FOR PAIRING WITH THE HALLOUMI.

RED VELVET COOKIES

INGREDIENTS

- 270G | 2 CUPS ALL-PURPOSE FLOUR
- 70G | ½ CUP DUTCH PROCESSED COCOA POWDER
- 1 TSP. BAKING SODA
- 1 TSP. SALT
- 200G | 1 CUP UNSALTED BUTTER
- 150G | ¾ CUP PACKED BROWN SUGAR
- 100G | ½ CUP GRANULATED SUGAR
- 1 LARGE EGG
- 1 TSP. RED GEL FOOD COLORING
- 2 TSP. PURE VANILLA EXTRACT
- 1 PACKET OF CHOCOLATE CHIPS

METHOD

SERVES 30 | **10 MINUTES PREP** | **15 MINUTES COOK**

STEP 01
IN A BOWL, ADD FLOUR, COCOA, BAKING SODA, AND SALT, AND WHISK TOGETHER.

STEP 02
IN ANOTHER BOWL, ADD BUTTER, BROWN SUGAR, AND GRANULATED SUGAR, THEN COMBINE USING A MIXER.

STEP 03
NOW ADD FOOD COLORING, EGG, AND VANILLA AND MIX THROUGH. ADD THE FLOUR MIXTURE AND WHISK WELL, THEN FOLD IN THE CHOCOLATE CHIPS.

STEP 04
CUT BAKING PAPER TO SIZE AND ADD TO THE AIR FRYER DRAWER, THEN ADD DOLLOPS OF THE MIXTURE ONTO THE PAPER USING A SPOON, SPACING THEM OUT (YOU MAY NEED TO BAKE IN BATCHES).

STEP 05
BAKE AT 150°C | 300°F FOR 14-15 MINUTES (OR UNTIL SLIGHTLY CRACKED ON TOP).

STEP 06
REMOVE IMMEDIATELY FROM THE AIR FRYER, AND ALLOW TO SET FOR 5 MINUTES.

CHOCOLATE CHIP COOKIES

INGREDIENTS

- ➤ 115G | 1/2 CUP UNSALTED BUTTER
- ➤ 100G | 1/2 CUP GRANULATED SUGAR
- ➤ 100G | 1/2 CUP BROWN SUGAR
- ➤ 1 EGG
- ➤ 1 TSP. PURE VANILLA EXTRACT
- ➤ 160G | 1 1/4 CUP PLAIN FLOUR
- ➤ 1/2 TSP. BAKING SODA
- ➤ PINCH SALT
- ➤ 175G | 1 CUP CHOCOLATE CHIPS

METHOD

 SERVES 4 10 MINUTES PREP | 08 MINUTES COOK

STEP 01 PREHEAT THE AIR FRYER TO 160 °C | 320°F.

STEP 02 CREAM TOGETHER YOUR BUTTER AND SUGAR UNTIL FLUFFY.

STEP 03 ADD THE EGG AND VANILLA AND BEAT WELL.

STEP 04 IN A SEPARATE BOWL, COMBINE FLOUR, BAKING SODA, AND SALT. GRADUALLY ADD THE WET INGREDIENTS.

STEP 05 SPOON ONLY PARCHMENT PAPER AND PLACE INTO YOUR AIR FRYER.

STEP 06 COOK FOR 6-8 MINUTES, OR UNTIL GOLDEN BROWN!

OAT PANCAKES

INGREDIENTS

- 100G | ¾ CUP OAT FLOUR
- ¾ TSP. BAKING POWDER
- ¼ TSP. SALT
- 1 LARGE EGG
- 125ML | ½ CUP WHOLE MILK
- 1 TBSP. BUTTER (MELTED)
- 1 TSP. MAPLE SYRUP
- ½ TSP. PURE VANILLA EXTRACT

METHOD

STEP 01
IN A BOWL, ADD BAKING POWDER, FLOUR, AND SALT THEN WHISK WELL.

STEP 02
IN ANOTHER BOWL, ADD MILK, BUTTER, EGG, SYRUP, AND VANILLA.

STEP 03
POUR THE FLOUR MIX INTO THIS BOWL AND FOLD IN WELL UNTIL COMBINED.

STEP 04
GREASE A PIE DISH LIGHTLY, THEN ADD ¼ OF THE BATTER.

STEP 05
ADD THE DISH INTO THE AIR FRYER AND COOK AT 200°C | 400°F FOR APPROX 3 MINUTES (OR UNTIL GOLDEN AND PUFFY).

STEP 06
REPEAT WITH THE REMAINING MIXTURE.

BANANA BLUEBERRY MUFFINS

INGREDIENTS

- 100G | ¾ CUP ALL-PURPOSE FLOUR
- 100G | ¾ CUP WHOLE WHEAT FLOUR
- 1 TSP. BAKING POWDER
- 1 TSP. BAKING SODA
- 3 LARGE OVERRIPE BANANAS
- 1 LARGE EGG
- 130G | ¾ CUP PACKED LIGHT BROWN SUGAR
- 80ML | ⅓ CUP VEGETABLE OIL
- 50G | ⅓ CUP SOUR CREAM
- 1 TSP. PURE VANILLA EXTRACT
- ¼ TSP. SALT
- 180G| 1 CUP BLUEBERRIES
- 14 BANANA CHIPS

METHOD

SERVES 14 | 10 MINUTES PREP | 15 MINUTES COOK

STEP 01 IN A BOWL, ADD BOTH TYPES OF FLOUR, BAKING POWDER, BAKING SODA, AND SALT.

STEP 02 IN ANOTHER BOWL, ADD BANANAS AND MASH WITH A FORK. ADD EGG, SUGAR, OIL, VANILLA, AND SOUR CREAM AND WHISK WELL.

STEP 03 ADD THE FLOUR MIX INTO THE BANANA MIX AND STIR WELL UNTIL COMBINED. ADD BLUEBERRIES AND FOLD INTO THE MIXTURE.

STEP 04 SCOOP THE MIXTURE EQUALLY INTO 14 MUFFIN CASES, AND TOP WITH 1 BANANA CHIP ON EACH.

STEP 05 ADD THE CASES TO THE AIR FRYER (YOU MIGHT NEED TO BAKE IN BATCHES), AND BAKE FOR 12-15 MINUTES AT 180°C | 350°F (ENSURING NOT TO BURN THE TOPS).

APPLE CRUMBLE

INGREDIENTS

- > 4 BRAMLEY APPLES (PEELED, AND SLICED - REMOVE CORE)
- > 4 TSP. GROUND CINNAMON
- > 50G | ¼ CUP DEMERARA SUGAR (PLUS 2 TBSP. FOR THE FILLING)
- > 100G | ½ CUP UNSALTED BUTTER
- > 200G | 1 ¼ CUPS PLAIN FLOUR

METHOD

 SERVES 6 10 MINUTES PREP | 30 MINUTES COOK

STEP 01
IN A CAKE TIN OR PIE DISH (ENSURE IT FITS THE AIR FRYER), PLACE THE APPLES AND POUR OVER 2 TBSP. WATER, 2 TSP. CINNAMON AND 2 TBSP. SUGAR, THEN MIX WELL.

STEP 02
AIR FRY THE APPLES AT 180°C | 350°F FOR 20 MINUTES, STIRRING WELL HALFWAY THROUGH.

STEP 03
IN A BOWL, ADD BUTTER AND FLOUR AND RUB TOGETHER UNTIL CRUMBLY. MIX THE REMAINING CINNAMON AND SUGAR TO THE MIX.

STEP 04
POUR THE CRUMBLE OVER THE COOKED APPLES AND EVEN THEM OUT (SO THE WHOLE SURFACE IS COVERED). AIR FRY FOR 10 MINUTES UNTIL PALE GOLD IN COLOR.

TOP TIP
WHY NOT SERVE WITH SINGLE CREAM OR CUSTARD?

POPCORN

INGREDIENTS

> 65G | 1/3 CUP POPCORN KERNELS

> YOUR SEASONING TOPPINGS OF CHOICE

METHOD

SERVES **2**

2 MINUTES PREP

08 MINUTES COOK

STEP 01
PREHEAT THE AIR FRYER TO 200°C | 390°F. ADD YOUR POPCORN KERNELS TO YOUR FOIL LINED AIR FRYER BASKET.

STEP 02
YOUR POPCORN KERNELS WILL NEED 8 MINUTES COOKING TIME. DON'T OPEN YOUR AIR FRYER BASKET FOR AROUND 30 SECONDS AFTER FINISHED COOKING TIME AS SOME KERNELS MIGHT STILL BE POPPING.

STEP 03
ONCE YOUR POPCORN IS READY, MIX IN A LARGE BOWL WITH YOUR PREFERRED SEASONINGS - THE POSSIBILITIES FOR SEASONINGS ARE ENDLESS. BE ADVENTUROUS AND FIND YOUR FAVORITE FLAVOR!

TOP TIP
WE LOVE:
BARBECUE: 1 TSP. SMOKED PAPRIKA, ¼ TSP. CAYENNE PEPPER, 1 TBSP. BROWN SUGAR
PUMPKIN SPICE: 1 TSP. GROUND CINNAMON, ¼ TSP. GROUND CLOVES, ½ TSP. GROUND GINGER.